Technology has shaped human life since the beginnings of civilization. In the 2005 Reith Lectures, Alec Broers shows how we owe to technologists most of what drives our world today. Using easily understood examples, he explains how today's remarkable technologies emerged, and conveys the excitement of the modern creative process that engages people all over the world. Having worked in both industry and universities, his views on their roles are strong, and he clearly recommends how they can best work together.

Alec Broers accepts that we need to understand technology's potential dangers, but is optimistic that this can be done. Worldwide collaboration will be needed, and a willingness on the part of the developed world to help the emerging world and to constrain its own use of limited resources. Only through technology, he argues, will we find solutions to the problems that threaten our planet.

LORD BROERS is President of the Royal Academy of Engineering and Chairman of the House of Lords Science and Technology Committee. He spent nineteen years in the research and development laboratories of IBM in the USA and then twenty years at Cambridge University as Professor of Electrical Engineering, Master of Churchill College, Head of the Engineering Department, and Vice-Chancellor. In his research at Cambridge and at IBM, he pioneered the use of electron beams to write the patterns for silicon chips.

The Triumph of Technology

ALEC BROERS

President
Royal Academy of Engineering

CAMBRIDGE
UNIVERSITY PRESS

CAMBRIDGE UNIVERSITY PRESS
Cambridge, New York, Melbourne, Madrid, Cape Town, Singapore,
São Paulo, Delhi, Dubai, Tokyo, Mexico City

Cambridge University Press
The Edinburgh Building, Cambridge CB2 8RU, UK

Published in the United States of America by Cambridge University Press, New York

www.cambridge.org
Information on this title: www.cambridge.org/9780521861588

First published 2005

A catalogue record for this publication is available from the British Library

ISBN 978-0-521-86158-8 Hardback
ISBN 978-0-521-67965-7 Paperback

CONTENTS

PREFACE

When the BBC originally approached me to discuss the possibility that I would deliver the Reith Lectures, my first thought was that I would speak about nanotechnology, my own field of engineering. But as I started to outline what I would say I found that I was repeatedly coming back to generalities, to the origins of technology and how the process of innovation has changed over time, especially over the last few decades. I was also influenced by my observation that the general public did not have a good understanding of this process, nor have a true appreciation of the benefits of modern technology. Worse than this, there was a growing distrust of technology and science that has its origins in a few isolated examples, but has spread to technology in general.

So my purpose in delivering the lectures was to make the case for technology, to show how technologies have, from the beginnings of civilisation, influenced the way we live and that, overall, they have been hugely beneficial. The standard of living of the majority of peoples has been improved to an extent that would have been inconceivable to our ancestors, and it is largely through technology that the peoples of the Third World will be able to enjoy the same privileges. I have tried to capture the wonder of modern technologies, setting them in a historical context but bringing a sense of reality to what they can accomplish. I also discuss the risks they pose and the need in some cases to limit their use.

I do not try precisely to define the words 'science', 'technology', 'engineering' and 'innovation', and in some cases I even use them interchangeably. I do so because I believe that this reflects reality. Scientists, engineers and innovators all use science, and all engineers and scientists innovate. It is difficult to distinguish when applied science becomes engineering, or indeed technology. My discussion of the development of the laser in Lecture 2 illustrates this point. However, my meaning should be clear because of the context in which I use the words. In Lecture 3, because I was not sure that any of these words would be adequate, I went through the text replacing the word 'innovation' with the words, 'product development', to ensure that there was no doubt that I was talking about the use of science – or is it engineering? – to produce useful products. Many engineers believe that it is engineering that makes science useful, but scientists will also claim to be doing this. I find this debate a waste of time. They both play a vital role.

The first lecture has the same title as the series, 'The Triumph of Technology'. I used 'Triumph' in the sense of 'success' not 'triumphalism'. I was aware that some would take the latter meaning and that this would fuel their fear of the influence of science and technology, but I retained the title because I felt that it had appropriately strong impact. Lecture 1 lays out my thesis for the series and my belief that, over all, technology has been of great benefit.

Lecture 2, 'Collaboration', discusses how modern technologies evolve, explaining how the process has become distributed and international, and how success lies in effective collaborations.

Lecture 3, 'Managing innovation', discusses the

ways in which the innovation process is managed and how, while products are still best developed by industry, the emphasis on basic research has moved from the large industrial research laboratories that emerged in the middle of the twentieth century, to universities.

Lecture 4, 'Nanotechnology and nanoscience', describes the broad range of technologies which have adopted the prefix 'nano' and discusses the potential for these archetypes of today's high-technology world.

Lecture 5, 'Risk and responsibility', is a broad ranging discussion of the risks posed by the increasing influence of technology and the responsibility we all carry in ensuring that they are managed responsibly. This final lecture ends with some speculation about what may emerge in the decades to come.

In the concluding section I have expanded and clarified some of the points made in the lectures, drawing upon the discussions that followed them – each of the lectures was delivered to a public audience and was followed by questions from the audience – and upon correspondence that I have received subsequently.

Lastly I would like to express my appreciation to Sue Lawley, Gwyneth Williams, Tony Phillips and the BBC team who put the broadcasts together. Sue Lawley introduced the lectures and skilfully guided the discussions and it is more than a coincidence that some of the topics I discuss could be considered as an extension of a brief exchange I had with Sue on *Desert Island Discs* in 2001. Gwyneth Williams is the Editor of the Reith Lectures, and Tony Phillips, the Senior Producer. Their professional and friendly help in adapting the texts for the somewhat unusual medium of a radio lecture were invaluable. I would also like to thank my colleagues in the Royal Academy of Engineering, and several of my friends, with especial mention of Geoffrey Skelsey, with whom I discussed the content of the lectures.

1

The triumph of technology

Around 4,000 years ago, just 5 miles north of what is now the Norfolk town of Thetford, our Neolithic ancestors began what may have been the largest early industrial process in these British Isles. This is the site that the Anglo-Saxons called 'Grimes Graves' and it contains nearly 400 mine-shafts built to extract high-quality flints, which could be chipped to produce sharp cutting edges. Using nothing but tools of bone and wood, and presumably the flints themselves, these ancient people excavated to a depth of up to 12 metres to reach the buried flints. It has been calculated that the miners needed to remove 1,000 tonnes of waste to produce 8 tonnes of flint. The site covers nearly 40 hectares and the whole project is astonishing.

Whilst more advanced technologies had developed elsewhere – for instance in China – our ancestors' task was anything but easy. They needed timbers to shore up their excavations and ladders to get down into them; lighting was required in the deeper pits and they needed tools, which they made from deer antlers, so they had to manage the local herds of red deer. A separate and skilled industry was required to work the extracted flints and to market and distribute them. The flints were used as axe-heads, as agricultural implements, as arrow-heads, and no doubt there were countless other applications that we have lost track of. The Grimes Graves operation underpinned the foundations of a new sort of society.

Humankind's way of life has depended on technology since the beginning of civilisation. It can indeed be argued that civilisation began when humans first used technologies, moving beyond the merely instinctual and into an era when people began to impose themselves on their environment, going beyond mere existence, to a way of life which enabled them to take increasing advantage of their intellect. A visit to Grimes Graves at its peak would have created as much wonder as was created by flight, or the telephone, when they first appeared.

Ranking in importance such early developments as

the techniques of flint extraction against subsequent developments, such as the use of metals, is not easy, especially as the primitive technologies were independently developed in widely separated societies. But any such ranking is fraught with difficulties. For example, a recent poll asked the British public how they would rank Britain's greatest inventions: electricity generation, which is the foundation of almost every current technology; the jet engine, which made possible our international mobility; the invention of vaccination that saved millions of lives; the discovery of the structure of DNA, which underpins biotechnology – the possibilities seemed endless. Well, the public chose none of these, but instead … the safety bicycle. And it was that choice which confirmed my subject for these lectures.

The bicycle is of course an ingenious, practical and sustainable invention, which brought new opportunities for people in every stratum of society, and which continues to offer benefits today. But to place it ahead of the fundamental accomplishments of Faraday, Stephenson, Maxwell, Thomson, Whittle, and Crick and Watson demonstrates in my mind a profound misunderstanding of the contribution of advanced technologies to our lives, and of the manner in which the vast pyramid of scientific and technical achievement that underlies these technologies was built.

The means to control plagues, to travel in hours to parts of the world which once took months to reach, to be able to access billions of written words from one's desk, to instantly conjure up high-quality images of distant objects and events – these are just a few of the technologies which we take almost for granted and which rest upon the accomplishments of generations of British engineers and scientists. Compared with these, I am afraid I cannot view the safety bicycle as a significant contender. But the fact that so many of our compatriots thought that it was of such paramount significance surely indicates a failure – of serious dimensions – in communication and understanding. I needed at least to try, in these lectures, to correct that failure.

My contention is that technology is sidelined and undervalued – we have become defensive about it and would rather retreat into the past, or into fundamental science, than strive to stay in the race. The cost of this major social failure will progressively disadvantage all of us. Technology is determining the future of the human race. We need it to satisfy our appetite for energy, perhaps through nuclear power; to help us address hunger throughout the world, through plant breeding; to monitor and find the means for avoiding global warming so that we can safeguard our planet for future generations. Technology can improve our health, and lengthen our lives. I want this lecture series to act as a wake-up call to all of us. Technology, I repeat, will determine the future of the human race. We should recognise this and give it the profile and status that it deserves.

The most straightforward explanation for the lack of appreciation is that modern technologies are too complex to be understood by anyone but the experts. But this is only true if the details are to be understood. It is up to the engineers and scientists who create these technologies to explain what they have done in language that can be understood by non-experts. We are very much to blame. Mind you, matters were no better in days gone by when those responsible for the developments were purposefully obscure about their discoveries. The boundary between science and what, for the sake of simplicity, we can call 'magic' was blurred. Even when the Royal Society, Great Britain's leading scientific academy, was founded in 1662, its objectives included matters we would now class as 'alchemy' rather than science. Knowledge was power and potentates were anxious to restrain its diffusion. Galileo was condemned and confined to house arrest for the latter part of his life for seeking to promulgate theories we now know to have been broadly correct. Worse perhaps than that, he wrote in the vernacular language (Italian) which could be understood by ordinary people, rather than the Latin of the scholars. And even the humdrum mining at Grimes Graves seems to have been associated with mystical rituals and ceremonies. The demystification of science is another change of the last few centuries, but it is evidently one which remains incomplete.

One of the reasons that the earliest significant advances were few and far between was that the technologies of communication had yet to be created, and communication of any kind could be rigidly controlled. While there was only word of mouth, information must frequently have been lost, and the process of innovation forced to repeat itself over and over again. Innovation could not build upon itself as it does today because there were no means to pass information reliably from generation to generation, or between widely separated societies. The difficulty of transportation compounded the problem: it was only the wealthy and powerful who could travel to distant sources of information. It was through primitive paintings and tablets of stone, and eventually hand-written manuscripts, that each generation first began to preserve and reliably to pass on its precious knowledge.

Progress remained slow because it was only through tedious hand copying that more than a single record could be produced, and replication in large numbers was impossible. It was the printing press that began to solve this problem. Printing was the first and perhaps the greatest of the communication technologies. It was followed four centuries later by the telegraph and then the telephone, the radio, the television and now, and perhaps as important in its influence as the early printing presses, the electronic media, especially the Internet. Electronic networks provide the ability to communicate instantaneously anywhere in the world and the World Wide Web [WWW] makes – in principle – all the information possessed by anyone available to everyone.

This previously inconceivable connectivity enables people to contribute to the process of innovation or, perhaps more importantly, to avoid the mistakes of others. Yet every advance in communication technology has facilitated the dissemination of both misinformation and disinformation; the more advanced the technology the greater the potential for misuse. The Internet is especially vulnerable as it is less controlled than its predecessors. The World Wide Web Consortium, an independent group at the Massachusetts Institute of Technology headed by Tim Berners-Lee (who is credited with first developing the WWW), is fighting to keep it this way for reasons I support, but the inevitable consequence is that it carries a plethora of falsehood, which any surf of the Web will speedily demonstrate. We must arm ourselves against such falsehood by teaching people to be intelligent critics and helping them to judge whether a source is reliable.

The ready availability of even objective truth does not mean that objective truth will be believed or absorbed. For example, the difficulty the public has in understanding science in some respects grows rather than shrinks in the age of unlimited information. This chapter was delivered as a lecture in the Royal Institution of London, 205 years old and specifically founded – mainly by non-scientists – to 'diffuse the knowledge, and to facilitate the general introduction, of useful mechanical inventions and improvements, and to teach the application of science to the common purposes of life'. Those rotund eighteenth-century phrases contain a mighty truth which we need to heed no less today.

Advances in technology accelerated as efforts to understand the world around us bore fruit. For instance, inherited folklore in medicine began to crumble in the light of advances in understanding made by William Harvey and others, based on systematic observation and recording. Harvey explained in the early 1600s that blood circulated around the body, pumped by the heart, rather than ebbing and flowing in the blood vessels. Newton put to flight so many of the myths about the universe. Newton's 'laws' introduced systematic and (on the face of things) simple rules which helped to explain the universe, and helped to solve previously insoluble problems. This was the beginning of a new era. Perversely, it was also when intellectual advances began to become so complex that it became difficult and eventually impossible for the non-specialist to understand them.

In the course of these chapters I shall look at some of the ways in which technologies have grown more complex, and yet how – despite hugely expanded public education – understanding of them has diminished. The idea of a straight-line development towards an ideal is attractive, but is alas untrue. There have been mistakes in judgement, mistakes some-times compounded by secrecy. In health-related issues there is the tragedy of thalidomide, to mention one example. Engineers, whilst making immense leaps in so many directions, have failed always to predict other consequences of operating in hitherto unknown regimes: the amazingly innovative British jet airliner, the Comet, ahead of all its competitors at the time, was aborted after a series of crashes caused by stress-induced fatigue. The engineers lacked sufficient knowledge of what turned out to be a deadly phenomenon.

Such lapses have tended to engender a sense of mistrust and suspicion on the part of the general public, and there is an ever more pressing need for scientists and engineers openly to communicate what they are doing and to be candid over the likely consequences of their work. This is a subject I will discuss at greater length in my final chapter when I will also examine our responsibilities towards the developing world.

I have found that the possession of an understanding of technology, just as with an understanding of music, literature or the arts, brings with it great personal satisfaction and pleasure. I still pause to wonder at the achievements of humankind, for example, when I am flying in comfort at 40,000 feet and look down on the white caps and spume of a turbulent sea so far distant below me, and realise the difficulties there were in crossing it only a couple of lifetimes ago. I know that I can safely drink the water that runs out of the tap in the majority of places I visit in the world, and can talk with my family or even hold in my hand a real-time picture of them wherever I am. How remarkable it is to gaze up at the moon and the planets and realise that we have already walked on that great sphere and have sent intelligent machines to those planets, even to their satellites, and received high-quality pictures and data from those remote surfaces.

My appreciation is all the greater because I know enough to realise how difficult it has been to accomplish these things, enough in fact to know how little – after a lifetime in science and engineering – I actually know myself. I sometimes play the game of wondering how much I would be able to recreate if by some cataclysmic disaster I were to be the only person left with knowledge of how these wonders were accomplished. I am afraid that it would only be a small and specialized fraction of electronics.

I was born in Calcutta. My father was an insurance

businessman, but his great passion was for technology, especially radio and photography. Indeed, he spent enough time on these hobbies for his expertise to be close to professional. His interest in radio is recorded in a series of articles that he wrote for the Calcutta *Statesman* in the late 1930s, discussing radio and reviewing the latest receivers. He was one of the first to receive the BBC on short-wave radio and he wrote under the pseudonym 'Superhet'. Radios and TVs still use superheterodyne receivers but that will have to be the subject of another series of lectures.

By happy coincidence, but perhaps not surprisingly, he wrote twice about Sir John Reith, describing him in 1938 as 'building up the BBC from its beginnings to the mighty machine which today transmits music, entertainment, and information to no less than 8,600,000 homes in Great Britain', and later pointing out that he had behaved as a virtual dictator in his management style. This was when he was about to leave the BBC to become Chairman of Imperial Airways.

That so many people were able to hear the lecture from which this chapter is transcribed is itself the consequence of a whole series of inventions and coincidences. Whilst some of the basic principles of radio were understood, the fundamental roots of broadcasting arrived partly by chance, as a technology thought of as the opportunity for 'messages without wires' turned unintentionally into a system of diffusion to multiple audiences. The development of the valve, 'the magic lamp of radio', was a decisive step, as I will describe in the next chapter, but so were the governmental and regulatory attitudes that followed and which for a time seemed likely to snuff out infant broadcasting.

No one could anticipate the effects of the radio, on the printed word, on politics, on social behaviour – even on advertising following that fateful day in 1922 when the first radio commercial was broadcast. The future US President, Herbert Hoover, said of this afterwards that it was 'inconceivable that we should allow so great a possibility for service ... to be drowned out by advertising chatter'. We all know what happened to that good intention, but at least the BBC and National Public Radio in the USA hold out against that chatter.

There was, you can be sure, no lack of commentators eager to predict the worst outcomes of radio broadcasting – that it would destroy theatres and newspapers, that it would vulgarise culture, things which either turned out to be untrue or were outweighed by the benefits. Through radio and, later, television, and subsequently the Internet, societies beyond the metropolitan circle – and beyond the 'rich' world – have access to music, literature, drama, information and news, in a way which was previously impossible.

Perhaps because we have yet to come fully to terms with their implications and possibilities, the potentialities of modern technology tend to be thought of in terms of such advances as those brought about by electronic communications and computers, and indeed those potentialities are awesome. But is it not developments in transport, medicine, energy and weaponry that have produced the greatest impact upon our lives?

It is surely by developments in medicine that the greatest numbers of the world's people have been most immediately affected. Changed techniques for travel have had revolutionary social consequences, at least in the First World. And some of the technologies of energy generation are threatening the planet's eco-system (and their profligate use of scarce non-renew-able resources presents still greater threats in the future). Finally, we are unlikely to overlook the impli-cations of weaponry and its delivery. These have shifted centres of power and have had unpredictable and as yet unforeseen effects on the relative success of different countries and societies. The twentieth century, during which so many advanced sciences were born, was also the century of previously unimaginable atrocities based on advances in tech-nology, and the capacity for yet greater atrocity clearly still exists.

I would argue, though, that most new technologies, with the exception of those associated with weaponry, have had hugely beneficial effects for most people, extending our capabilities and indeed our lives to an extent that our ancestors could not have imagined, and I believe that we are only at the beginning.

We began this chapter in the empty landscape of East Anglia, four millennia ago. The basis of the highest achievement in their day, flints were superseded as a fundamental technology by metals of increasing sophistication. Now they are but historic artifacts. Other, far more complex, technologies have followed a similar course, passing from the mainstream into recreation, heritage and history. One thinks of the sailing ship and the steam locomotive, although Ellen MacArthur's heroic sailing triumph suggests that technological developments in sailing are alive and well.

The cycle of technological change grows faster. Compared with the sailing ship how brief was the longevity of the steam engine, let alone the vinyl gramophone record. What will be the next cycle, and how will it emerge? I hope it is clear by now that I am convinced that it is technology that shapes our lives and that its influence is paramount and is only going to increase as time passes. It is time for us in Britain, so good at fundamental science, also to come fully to appreciate the intellectual challenge behind product development. We seem culturally unable to realise that this can be more challenging than the fundamental science and requires the very best minds. In my view this has already been grasped in India and China, which is pleasing because, after all, technology is the means by which the developing world can increase its standard of living. If we do not join the race to advance technology we face serious consequences – not least, that we will fall behind in our own intellectual, social and material development.

2

Collaboration

When I returned to Cambridge University's Engineering Department from the USA in 1984, my wife and I bought a historic and wonderful house some ten miles south of Cambridge. It was built around 1520, a date that could be substantiated to within a decade by the form of the oak beams that comprised its floors and ceilings. These had been shaped by iron blades that only lasted about ten years. Being someone of the present rather than the past I had not previously been much preoccupied with history, but living in the splendid oak structure – like a fine sailing vessel that had gone aground – inspired me to wonder what had preoccupied the technologists and scientists of that age.

In my search I discovered that on 24 August 1563 a 'conjunction' took place of the planets Saturn and Jupiter. The two appeared so close together in the sky that they seemed to merge together. This rare occurrence was of great importance in an era when it was widely believed that exceptional astronomical events both influenced and predicted worldly happenings.

The problem was that the very best minds of the period, in Europe at least, were quite unable to calculate exactly when the conjunction was to take place. Some calculations were at least a month out. The best were inaccurate by days. Given the science and technology of the period, such inaccuracy is easy to understand. There were no reliable and accurate clocks. And without astronomical telescopes, robust celestial observation was to a great extent impossible. And besides, how many of us could do this calculation today?

The importance of overcoming such problems was not just a matter of shoring up the credibility of astrologers. Upon fine and accurate astronomical observation, and upon accurate timekeeping, depended reliable navigation, and the possibility of fruitful voyaging in the coming centuries. Measurement, the development of observational instruments and accurate clocks, complex calculations: all these came together in the ensuing centuries. This effective marriage between science and technology produced remarkable advances in navigation. Governments, and private enterprises and individuals, enthusiastically joined in this endeavour, which ultimately produced the Global Positioning System, which I shall describe later, and its European descendant Galileo.

We think of such support as a modern phenomenon, but in fact – in Europe at least – governments have supported scientific and technological research for centuries. Such support was commonly tied to the fulfilment of contemporary needs, for example in the development of accurate systems of navigation to overcome the shortcomings we have just glimpsed.

Most modern technologies are created by bringing together and developing capabilities which already exist. The genius lies in the way they are brought together and improved. There are innumerable examples to illustrate the process. The long-sought mobile phone was made a reality by bringing together mathematical concepts of cellular networks, advanced ultra-high-frequency radios, low-power microprocessors, and improved batteries. The mobile phone was not invented, although buried within it are innumerable inventions, and several of the geniuses who design the world's best cell-phones do so just south of Cambridge. The hybrid car combines the efficient modern internal combustion engine with pollution-free electric drive and systems that recycle the energy dissipated in braking. The modern jet airliner combines innumerable individual capabilities in mechanical design, aerodynamics, jet engines, electronic communication and navigation systems, and the airports that they serve are wonders of modern civil engineering. Other examples easily come to mind: the modern dental surgery, flat-screen TVs, medical scanners, the ubiquitous scanning electron microscope developed in the Cambridge University Engineering laboratory, electronic stock exchanges, Dyson's vacuum cleaner, the apparatus used to decode DNA, the iPod, and so on. All of these new technologies came about through a process in which established capabilities were evolved and combined in new ways. They were the result of engineers seeking solutions to practical problems and human need. They did not emerge from basic science.

When fundamentally new materials or ideas are available the potential is even greater, but the route to useful products is longer and therefore the commercial risks are higher. Such is the case, for example, with the polymer semiconductors that have emerged recently in the Cavendish laboratory that offer no less than a revolution in computer displays and in low-cost electronics.

In this second chapter, I explore the origins of modern technologies. I believe that today collaboration is essential for success because it brings both global awareness and the ability to gather together diverse capabilities. It is rare that individuals or groups working in isolation possess all that is needed. During my time at Cambridge I concentrated on extending the bridges that provided global awareness and enabled collaborations – with industry, with universities, with government. Without joining with others, one quite simply does not have the resources to be internationally competitive; nor does one have the 'spirit level' that reveals whether or not one is even in the race – complacency and smugness easily set in.

Mind you, there are dangers in collaboration, especially in the security of ideas – patents can protect ideas but necessarily give away the details when they are published. Individuals have this dilemma. They need to be a part of the larger world and communicate with it, but the moment they reveal their ideas, they have to be ready to run fast or competitors will out-speed them. I will return to this question in the third chapter.

The process of collaboration has been vastly enhanced by modern communications. The World Wide Web, which Tim Berners-Lee originally developed to allow physicists to work together, now allows creators of technology in every corner of the earth to work together – or to compete. And it is amazing how the efforts of creative engineers lead to advances and novel concepts that could not have been imagined by those who carried out the original research.

Which brings me to the laser. Few now remember that the laser was an adaptation of the earlier maser. The maser, an acronym for Microwave Amplification by Stimulated Emission of Radiation, was a device devised by Charles Townes to meet the need for an electronic oscillator that would operate at very high radio frequencies. It was an electronic device. Townes proposed that a similar device should be possible that operated at optical frequencies, and two years later Theodore Maiman demonstrated the first laser. The laser uses the same principles as the maser but operates at optical frequencies, hence the acronym Light Amplification by Stimulated Emission of Radiation.

It was predicted in 1960, when the laser was first demonstrated, that it would revolutionise optical imaging systems and make holograms feasible, but no one could have imagined the breadth of applications that were to emerge. No one could have foreseen that lasers would be used to transmit the majority of the world's telephone and television signals, or to record and play back sound and vision using plastic disks, let alone the plethora of other applications that now benefit everyone. These were subsequent accomplishments of technologists.

Telephone and television, and indeed all forms of electronic communications, are now carried around the world by beams of light that are channelled down glass fibres. The light beams are generated and modulated by solid state lasers that are so fast that a single beam can, for example, carry tens of thousands of simultaneous phone calls. A metal wire can carry about a hundred. An essential component in these optical systems is the Erbium amplifier which allows the light signal to be amplified directly without first converting it back to an electronic signal. This key advance was made by British engineers.

The technology of optical communication had its earliest origins in science but through most of its development it was a technologist's technology progressing through a series of intellectual advances that outweigh those of the original researchers. The achievements have been extraordinary – it has connected the world in a way that engineers would have thought impossible thirty years ago and avoided a log-jam in the Internet that people predicted twenty years ago.

These advances involved many people in many laboratories. One model says that ten times the effort needed in the original research must be expended in developing a prototype technology, and ten times this effort is needed to produce the manufactured product. The idea that a single person can 'invent' a new technology is out of the question in these cases. Creative ideas, of course, come from individuals, but their ideas must fit into the matrix of creativity being generated by individuals and teams all over the world.

I have discussed only two of the unexpected applications of the laser. I could have told similar stories about its applications to materials processing, such as the re-shaping of the lenses in our eyes, high-quality welding, or precision measurement. Even some of the humble and reliable printing devices attached to our home computers apply low-power lasers in an unforeseen manner. The successful applications of the laser far exceed the most extravagant predictions made in the 1960s.

The process of improving existing capabilities and adapting them to new applications relies on something that we do not need to teach, something that is inherent in the way the best technologists operate. Creative engineers are, by nature, problem solvers, always seeking ways to employ advances in technology in new and better ways. It is an extraordinarily exciting activity. Look back to the era of the first European ocean voyagers: the lack of reliable time-keepers to determine longitude, the reliance on crude devices such as the cross-staff to make astronomical observations. The navigators' achievements were astonishing, but consider where we are by contrast today.

GPS, the Global Positioning System, because it built on the vast technological achievements of humankind, belittled previous accomplishments. GPS had its origins almost exclusively in technology. It uses principles related to those of land-based navigational systems but with the signals coming from satellites rather than ground-based transmitters.

The idea of building a satellite-based location system emerged when a number of quite separate developments coincided. The cost of launching satellites became finite; advances in microelectronics allowed the necessary electronics to be packed into a small satellite and the receivers to be compact and reasonably priced; and finally, it was seen that such a system could have military significance making available the billions of dollars necessary to put up the twenty three satellites. This technology grew out of space research and microelectronics and was funded by the military.

At the time it was decided to build the Global Positioning System, I suspect that few would have foreseen that within a decade tens of millions of receivers would be sold and that they would not just be used for navigating ships and planes. Farmers would use them to guide their tractors, taxi fleets would be managed using GPS data, the arrival of trains and buses would be announced, and authorities would keep track of criminals on parole with GPS ankle bracelets. Standard cars would carry GPS-based navigational systems and these would not only tell people where they were, but, just as importantly perhaps, the location of the nearest Indian restaurant.

But stop to wonder a moment about this technology. A GPS receiver contains up to a dozen individual receivers, each of which automatically searches the frequency spectrum to find the tiny synchronised signals from the satellites. The receiver's computer knows the exact position of each satellite, and from the time delay between the signals it calculates its own position in three dimensions to an accuracy of a few metres. A modern receiver takes a few seconds to locate the satellites, make these measurements, and fix its position. And less than five centuries ago, humankind could not even reliably predict a rare astronomical event.

In 1992 I had the privilege of visiting one of the Royal Navy's nuclear submarines. It had an electronic navigation system that performed similar functions. It occupied an entire six-foot-high rack of electronics, cost a large fraction of a million pounds, and took five minutes to give a fix with an accuracy of a few hundred metres. One of today's hand-held GPS receivers gives a ten times more accurate fix in a hundredth of the time at one ten-thousandth of the cost. This is a triumph of technology.

To create technologies like GPS, and indeed to make progress in any advanced technology, engineers must be familiar with the full spectrum of technologies and know what is hindering further progress. To do this they must be working at the frontiers of development. If they are not, then they cannot concentrate their resources efficiently and their efforts will not be competitive. Working from first principles is not effective as it opens up too many alternatives.

Obviously, progress is most rapid when the factors impeding progress are known. This does not make the problems easy to solve, and indeed with most modern technologies the solution generally requires an intimate knowledge of the science that underpins the technology, but without knowledge of these factors focus is lost. Let me trace the evolution of electronics as another example.

Electronics began with J. J. Thomson's identification of the electron in Cambridge in 1897. One could go back even earlier and seek the origins of scientific methodology but let me start at the time that Thomson proposed that the 'rays' which Europe's physicists had been experimenting with for many years were in fact streams of sub-atomic particles, 'corpuscles', later called 'electrons'. J. J. Thomson used a glass bottle in which he had embedded a cathode from which the electrons would emerge, and an anode that attracted them. This was in effect a primitive cathode ray tube as used in television sets although there was in fact some residual gas in the bottle and there were ions as well as electrons, but the simple analogy is none the less useful.

This primitive electron tube was adapted a few years later by John Fleming and used as a 'detector' for weak electromagnetic signals in the earliest experiments in long-range radio transmission, that had been pioneered by Marconi. Fleming's diode was complemented by the triode of De Forest. The electron current in De Forest's triode flowed through a third electrode, called the grid, and a small signal applied to the grid produced a large change in the current and therefore the signal at the anode. De Forest's triode amplified the tiny signal from Fleming's diode, making radio as we know it possible. The triode was the first of a family of devices known as 'vacuum valves' in the UK and 'vacuum tubes' in the USA. The technology of electronics had been born and it was vacuum valves that gave rise to most of the electronic systems that we are familiar with today, including computers. But engineers were not satisfied with the valve, and following the Second

World War a search for a better alternative began, which eventually led to the transistor.

The first transistor was developed by John Bardeen, Walter Brattain and William Shockley at Bell Telephone Laboratories in New Jersey in December of 1947. They were seeking an alternative to the vacuum valve that was cheaper, lower-power and less fragile: an electronic device that operated like the valve but did not have to operate in a vacuum. Their device turned out to be perhaps the most important single technological development of the twentieth century; but these three pioneers could never have imagined what was to come. By early in the twenty-first century, more transistors would have been built than characters printed since the beginning of time. I will bring this story up to date in the fourth chapter when I will discuss nanotechnology.

After the contribution of J. J. Thomson, who was clearly motivated by the desire to understand the universe, the development of electronics followed the route of most successful technological developments. The engineers and scientists who made the remarkable breakthroughs were not being driven by science and a wish to understand nature – their aim was to find useful applications for their knowledge.

Today, the fledgeling electronics, that started with the elementary three-electrode valve, has reached extremes. A chip-manufacturing plant costs several billion dollars and if you have problems that delay the production of a new chip for six months you may have lost 50 per cent of the profit from that chip. And this industry is not alone in its magnitude and complexity. The situation is similar in many other fields, certainly in aerospace and in the automobile industries, and the resources needed to be successful in the pharmaceutical industry are just as great and the adherence to schedule even more critical.

By now it should be clear why it is not only difficult but impossible to make progress in this sort of high technology if you are not already at the frontiers of development. If you are not, then you have no means of knowing where to concentrate your efforts. It is possible with a relatively small team to tackle new technologies, but only if the team is fully aware of the international competitive situation and is linked in with partners that have the ability to proceed at a competitive pace. There can be no half-hearted commitment.

Advances equivalent to those of past centuries are extremely unlikely to be achieved in the same way today, by the separate endeavours of often amateur researchers and technologists. James Joule, working in a private laboratory attached to his father's brewery; Michael Faraday, brought up as a bookbinder's apprentice and educated through studying the books that passed through his hands; Thomas Newcomen, an ironmonger and blacksmith: these and other giants of past ages made their achievements partly alone and largely by happy chance. Such a course is probably impossible today, but the excitement and thrill of achievement are just the same. There are few more satisfying activities than the creation of new technologies for the benefit of humankind. Creative engineers may not receive the recognition they deserve in this country but it rarely troubles them – the satisfaction they derive from their jobs is unsurpassed.

3

Managing innovation

When Ralph Waldo Emerson reputedly and memorably said that the world would beat a path to the door of a person who made a better mousetrap, he was perhaps being unduly optimistic, but at least he realised that the mousetrap had to be made and that it would not be sufficient merely to have an idea, or even a patent, for a better mousetrap. Ideas have to be proven to be useful, and the world told about them, before any paths are beaten. Profound changes have taken place in the development of ideas and their translation into the marketplace, and in this third chapter I argue that this innovation revolution demands a new approach to research and product development.

To illustrate this story I go back to the beginning of my research career. I was drawn to Britain from the sunshine of Australia in 1959 because Britain led the

world in making the best domestic electronics, especially the high-fidelity sound systems that had fasci-
nated me since I was a boy. I had formed a little
company in Melbourne – today we would call it a
'start-up' – that made hi-fi systems for rich farmers,
and all the equipment that we used was British,
including the electronic components, so my ambi-
tion was to come to England and work on their
further development.

But by the time I had finished my Ph.D. in 1965, the
excitement in electronics had moved to transistors
and the newly emerging integrated circuits, and my
Ph.D. research had taken me strongly in this direc-
tion. Some of the important concepts for integrated
circuits had emerged in Britain, in particular at the
Royal Signals and Radar Establishment in Malvern,
but the most exciting research was being pursued in
the laboratories of the large American technology
companies. There was a great demand for Ph.D.
graduates in electronics and related fields and the
'brain drain' from the UK to the USA was at full flow.

There was no doubt in anybody's mind at that time
that the ideal model for technology development was

the large, well-funded, industrial research laboratory staffed with talented Ph.D. graduates from the world's leading universities. Fundamental research could go on in universities but it was only in the large industrial or government-funded research laboratories that the really important practical advances were made. If I wanted to work on the creation of new technologies – on the evolution of the better mousetrap – then I would have to go to such a laboratory. This was the case not only in computers and communication but in the transport, chemical and pharmaceutical industries also.

The most famous of the industrial research laboratories was the great A.T.&T. Bell Telephone Laboratory that had dominated the world of communications for decades, but there were many other fine laboratories. General Electric, Hewlett Packard, Hughes Aircraft, Westinghouse, General Motors, and so on, all maintained large research facilities and relied on them to provide the ideas and technologies for their new products. I chose the new IBM Research Laboratory because IBM led in computer technology and they were running some projects where I could apply my Ph.D. research directly. And besides, the IBM laboratory was housed in a magnificent new Eero Saarinen building surrounded by seventy acres of beautiful grounds in the country fifty minutes north of New York City and everyone was talking about it. As I have said, this was the era when the industrial research laboratories dominated the world of technological research.

But that was forty years ago and much has changed since then, and it is the way things have changed that I discuss in this chapter. The domination of the large industrial research laboratory has largely come to an end, and, in all fields except perhaps pharmaceuticals, those that remain no longer operate in the same manner. They have become far more focussed on product development. It is the way this has happened, and what has replaced these large institutions which once seemed so dominant and impregnable, that interests me.

Industrial research laboratories were, and are, extraordinarily expensive, and, to an extent, speculative. The payback is the new products that they enable. Their task is to take advances in science, or novel uses and combinations of existing technologies, and demonstrate that they can be used to produce useful commercial products. In the larger companies the research laboratories were not required to produce finished products – that was left to 'development' laboratories – their task was to demonstrate that it was in principle possible to make the product. But they did much more than this. They were also charged with carrying out fundamental research to underpin the activities of the parent company. They provided the reservoir from which most, if not all, of the fundamental advances from which products were to be developed would be drawn.

By no means all innovative research carried out in industrial laboratories succeeded commercially – who has now heard of Remington-Rand computers? Neither was everything taken up by the parent company – the ubiquitous icons that we see on personal computer screens were first proposed by workers in Xerox's research laboratory and yet Xerox never made computers in large volumes. But up until the 1980s it was the industrial research laboratories that acted as the well-springs from which most successful new products were drawn.

In addition to providing the scientific underpinning to a range of products, researchers were rewarded for making contributions to fundamental science, even if it was unrelated to the company's business. I remember scientists in the IBM Research Laboratory working on gravity waves, the formation of galaxies, and fractals, subjects of importance to science, but that bore little relation to IBM's products. Achievements in science were considered as important as solutions that enabled new products to be successful.

In retrospect it becomes obvious that this support of fundamental science was in effect a philanthropic activity, and could be afforded because the companies that practised it on a significant scale were in fact monopolies. Some thought that they owed it to society. This has now changed. Very little fundamental research remains in corporate research laboratories.

The world has become more competitive and there are now few, if any, companies in any country that exercise an effective monopoly. The world of technology and science has also expanded so much that it is no longer possible, even for the largest companies, to sustain a research effort that can cover all the disciplines used in their products. Finally, leading research is going on all over the world and it is less and less likely that the important new ideas will emerge in a company's own laboratory. It is better to put in place mechanisms that draw on the global research output, which incidentally is no longer confined to Europe, Japan and North America but is emerging rapidly in China and India. The aim must be to draw upon the entire world of science and technology.

So, given this transformation, where is it best to pursue basic research and how should companies manage and organise the creation of new products? It is relatively easy to answer the first of these questions. Fundamental research is best carried out in universities. Universities allow researchers to set long-range goals – they are free to further humankind's understanding of the universe. This also makes them good at the type of research that used to be the domain of the industrial research laboratory. They have critical mass through the support of governments and can sustain breadth across the disciplines including the social sciences, and in some cases also the arts and humanities. Successful academics are active participants in the international community and are in a position to discuss their work without constraint with their peers around the world. They live in an environment that is continually refreshed by the intake of new students, and, provided the faculty are motivated to remain active in areas of current interest, they remain agile and creative. It is the scope and variety of interdisciplinarity and the constant renewal brought by new, young minds which underpin the achievements of university research. Government-funded research laboratories are also in a good position to sustain strong fundamental research, although they are more likely to lose creativity as their membership ages.

The principal challenge for any research organisation, when their aim is to pursue research which underpins technology, is to find ways to transfer their ideas into practical advances – in other words to be effective in technology transfer. This is especially the case for universities. Universities have made significant advances in recent years through the setting up of what are called 'incubators' and by supporting work that takes ideas to the point of initial feasibility. They have shown that they can be effective in providing the input to the product development process, especially when new scientific concepts are involved.

When it comes to product development, however, academics have difficulty in being sufficiently single-minded. They have to teach and examine, and tend nowadays to be evaluated on their output of original research. The product development process, on the other hand, requires focussed dedication to product aims. Important scientific advances are made along the path to the product but these usually become valuable intellectual property and their creators will not be motivated, or even allowed, to publish them. Academics who have been involved in the research phase of technology development, however, make valuable consultants and their involvement in the product development process is hugely beneficial.

The creation of new products is therefore only effectively carried out by dedicated teams who can devote 100 per cent of their time to the activity. To be successful the innovators will almost certainly need an intimate knowledge of the science that underlies the technology, but their aim will not be to further the science. They will use their knowledge to break down the barriers that stand in the way of practical application. The resources needed to innovate are typically greater than those needed in research. As Thomas Edison famously said, the process is 'one per cent inspiration and ninety-nine per cent perspiration', and the energy and effort called for to take the idea of our better mousetrap successfully through to the sales floor is immense. This is partly because the process becomes a race against competitors, and the team must be large enough to get to their goal in time; and partly because there is an overriding need to demonstrate that there are reliable means to manufacture the product in high volumes.

Although there will be different ways to organise the creation of products in different industries, some general needs can be identified. Innovation today is global, so innovators must be familiar with what is going on all over the world – they should be members of the international community in their subject, or at least be in close contact with those who are, such as leading academics. For large companies with adequate resources this can be accomplished through collaborative research programmes with universities. In such programmes the goals of the research should be jointly set by the academics and industrialists so that everyone is familiar with the needs of the product or process programmes as well as with the research agenda. Such joint projects are also effective in transferring technology that has had its origins in universities. It is not effective for industry merely to 'contract out' their research needs to universities.

In small and medium-sized companies, where the resources are not great enough to fund large-scale research in universities, technology is best transferred by the academics moving out of their universities and devoting their full energies to the product development process. Many venture capitalists require this before they will fund a start-up. If they are not prepared to devote full-time to the project themselves they will have to find others who will, and then act as advisors. This is not the best way to do things but it is a common model.

It is also important to realise that the original ideas of the founding entrepreneurs usually only form the core of what will be required. The rest of the creative input will have to come from all over the world. It is therefore important for small companies to be in touch with all sources of expertise; with universities, large companies, government-funded establishments, etc. – feeding off their ideas and using the larger organisations' resources to lever their own activities. In recent years in Britain it has been the small companies that have worked alongside large companies in a complementary way – such as ARM whose microprocessors power more than three-quarters of the world's mobile phones – that have succeeded. Competing with the technological giants head-on normally ends in failure, or in selling out at their terms as they have the ability to dominate the small company's sector of the market should they choose to do so.

To understand the degree to which product development has changed and become global, one only has to examine the aerospace, mobile telephone or automobile industries. The components that make up these systems are no longer made by single companies. Technologies are brought together from around the world and integrated into the final product. The indispensable modern cellular telephone drew on technology developed in Finland, Sweden, Japan and the USA, and many of the most advanced phones are designed in the UK. The components of a modern airliner like the Airbus 380 have been drawn from hundreds of locations in Europe, the USA and the Far East, as are the components of modern cars. The innovation is distributed and international, and perhaps the most powerful minds of all are those at the centre who have to decide which technologies to select and how they will be brought together. The situation is similar in the chemical and pharmaceutical industries and in the building of large computer software systems.

In cases where the product is to be mass-produced, as with most consumer products, the development of a commercially competitive manufacturing process is similarly global and takes even greater resources. And again there is an interface, this time between development and manufacturing, where collaboration and the transfer of people is once more the key to success. As already mentioned, the resources needed to develop the manufacturing process can be 10 times greater than those in development, or 100 times those in research.

Throughout all of what I have been talking about, the handling of intellectual property is key. The intellectual property must be sound and the ownership of patents clear and capable of withstanding challenge. Multiple ownership makes patents difficult to manage internationally and should, if possible, be avoided. Professionalism is essential. This is not the territory of the gifted amateur, even if many still cling to this romantic idea. Losing one's own and everyone else's money through unprofessional protection of intellectual property is not romantic.

Leadership in the creation of new technology is of prime importance and nobody will be surprised to hear that there are tensions between the ambitions of creative engineers who would rather publish their results and gain recognition than wait for patents, the demands of the market, and the availability of resources. This is one area where the vast increase in the technology base and the spreading of this base around the globe has not changed things. I believe that technology-based businesses should always be led by those who understand and have most experience of the market. Creative technologists provide the ideas for the new products and the expertise for manufacturing them, and may of necessity have to carry a new company through its early stages, but only the exceptional amongst them are able to develop a realistic view of the market for their ideas.

In a small company, the ideal leadership team consists of a chief executive who has extensive experience of the market and good business sense, the creative engineer who stands at the chief executive's right hand and provides knowledge and contacts that spread throughout the entire technical spectrum, and the chief financial officer who acts as the disciplinarian. In large companies the team should retain the same characteristics and hierarchy, although the capabilities will be distributed over the layers of the organisation. What has changed over the last few years is that everyone now has to have an international perspective, and preferably international working experience.

The world of product and process creation has become wholly international. To be only nationally competitive is to be uncompetitive. The pace has also accelerated to the extent that those who do not thrive in a stressful environment had better find something else to do. In the oft-quoted words of Andy Grove, the past head of Intel: 'Only the paranoid survive.' He was not using 'paranoid' in the sense used by psychiatrists, he was saying that one had to be prepared to expect anything from one's competitors. This is a fast-moving and ultra-competitive world. In the last decade of the twentieth century, we lived through what was in effect a new industrial revolution. Companies ceased to make entire products themselves and became assemblers of the world's best, and to do this they had to know the world – both its technologies and its peoples. And these trends are only going to accelerate as the emerging powers of India and China enter the world of innovation as powerfully as they entered high-technology manufacturing. It is immensely exhilarating to be a player, but there are no places reserved for amateurs.

4

Nanotechnology and nanoscience

Since time immemorial, people have been entranced by structures of great size. From the Colossus of Rhodes and the Great Pyramid, themselves no mean technical achievements, to the mighty Cunard 'Queens' built in Glasgow, and whichever is transiently the tallest building in the world, beholders have gaped in awe at the gigantic. One simple attraction has been that of comparative scale: so many times the size of a man, or a horse or of Nelson's Column, as popular illustrations used to show. It was easy for the bystander immediately to apprehend the vast size of these objects.

In some of these instances, big was beautiful: the sole purpose of size was to inspire awe. But, increasingly, in other cases there was an important practical purpose, the superior functionality of a large steamship or aircraft, for instance, which would outperform its smaller rivals. Starting with that greatest of engineers, I. K. Brunel, increase in size, whether of ships or railway locomotives, became an important technical aspiration.

We had to wait for the age of electronics, however, for miniaturisation to become an important achievement in its own right – until the same kind of awe could be inspired by the very small. Over the centuries artisans painstakingly wrote prayers on the heads of pins, painted portraits so small that the detail is scarcely discernible, and carved ivory figures so tiny that one can but marvel at the dexterity of the sculptors. Collectors treasured these works as examples of remarkable human skill, but few if any practical applications were found for them, and to most people they were, quite literally, invisible. Even in our great-grandparents' day, the most advanced technology easily accessible to ordinary people was probably the pocket watch, in its day a triumph of miniaturisation.

Electronics changed all of this. Electronics becomes better and more useful in almost every respect as it is miniaturised. Less than a lifetime ago, radio technology was awkward and cumbersome partly because it relied on vacuum valves to amplify the tiny radio signals. These 'valves' were not only bulky and fragile but they needed heat in order to work, so that a source for that heat was required, and the system had to be cooled. As I have already discussed in an earlier chapter, the development of the transistor after the Second World War changed all of that. Beginning with the original point-contact transistor, a family of devices was developed which superseded the thermionic valve, because they were faster, cheaper, and consumed less energy. Crucially, they were also smaller, so much so that eventually thousands of millions of them could be crowded on to a piece of silicon no larger than a postage stamp. When this vast assembly of electronic switches is brought into action, its computational power rivals that of the human brain. It is a technology that has changed the way we live.

In my view, this was the original thread in the tapestry that has become nanotechnology and nanoscience. There are now dozens of threads of many colours that have been woven into this tapestry, and in this fourth chapter I explore their origins and articulate a view about this suddenly so fashionable branch of science and technology. As in the history of any human endeavour, the weaving of the tapestry has not been without diversions and distractions and some of the more extravagant and exaggerated threads have had to be unpicked. I will also use the relationship between nanotechnology and nanoscience to illustrate the more general relationship between science and technology. It is rich with examples of the different ways in which scientists and technologists are motivated and go about their professions.

As I have said, the founding thread was the electronic chip. The concept of the chip emerged in the late 1950s when it was first realised that it would be possible to integrate all the elements of an electronic circuit onto a single piece of silicon. As a result, it was no longer necessary slavishly to follow the route that had been used with valve electronics, where circuits were built up with physically separated components, that were linked together with wires. Instead it became possible to fabricate all the elements simultaneously in a single piece of silicon using 'microlithography', a process that had its roots in the art of lithography. Microlithography is used first to fabricate the transistors in the silicon and then to pattern the multilayer maze of wires on top of the transistors that interconnect them. For the first two decades of this miniaturisation revolution, the prefix 'micro' seemed adequate, but when we managed to make an 8-nanometre (a nanometre is one billionth of a metre or about five times the diameter of an atom) wire at IBM in 1976, and even wrote 'USA 1976' in 10-nanometre gold letters, we decided that it was time to replace 'micro', or one millionth, with 'nano' meaning one billionth. The electron beam method we used was derived from one that I had used in Cambridge in the early 1960s to make 50-nanometre metal structures. It would have taken about 100 million of the 8-nanometre diameter wires to form a cable the size of a human hair and we decided that the term 'microlithography' was no longer adequate, so we introduced the term 'nanolithography'. This was the first technology to adopt the 'nano' prefix.

Initially we said that to be a 'nanostructure' the structure had to be smaller than 10 nanometres, but over the years, because too few useful artificial structures of this size were made, the definition was relaxed to 100 nanometres. The early nanostructures were not used in integrated circuits because nobody knew how to design a transistor that small. In fact for many years it was thought that transistors would not operate satisfactorily when their dimensions were reduced below a micron, or 1,000 nanometres, but these pessimists proved resoundingly wrong. In a modern transistor, the 'gate length', which is approximately the distance the electrons have to travel, is only about 40 nanometres.

Although the nanostructures were not immediately useful to integrated circuits, there was a surge of interest in them because they allowed quantum phenomena to be observed – in other words, they were so small that electrons passing through them behaved as waves as well as particles and it was hoped that this behaviour might be useful in devices – and naturally the techniques used to make them were also used by those exploring the limits of transistor fabrication. One of the leading laboratories in the world in this field, especially in the fabrication of very fast transistors, is at Glasgow University.

The wonderful progress that has been made in miniaturizing electronics, and which was predicted by Gordon Moore[1] forty years ago, has now reached the point where 'microelectronics' has become 'nanoelectronics', and electronic chips are now without doubt amongst the most useful of the nanotechnologies.

The second thread that makes up the nanotechnology tapestry had its origin in 1981 in the development of the scanning tunnelling microscope, known as the STM, a striking new scientific instrument that won its creators, Gerd Binnig and Heinrich Rohrer, a share in the 1986 Nobel Prize in Physics. The STM, and a number of instruments that operate in a similar way, are simple in concept but have proved capable of producing immense quantities of original scientific data about surfaces and molecules, and a version of the STM was used in the late 1980s to produce the ultimate in nanofabrication – the placement of single atoms. The STM truly works at the nanoscale and the

1   Gordon Moore was co-founder of the Intel Corporation with Robert Noyce. He predicted in 1965 that the number of components on silicon chips would double every year, an estimate that, in the amended form of a doubling every year and a half or so, would become known as Moore's Law.

scientific information it produced comprises the oeuvre that became 'nanoscience'.

The scanning tunnelling microscope consists of a tiny metal wire that is scanned across the surface to form an image – in the same way that the spot scans across the screen to form a television image, but more slowly. The tip is brought so close to the surface that electrons tunnel across the gap, and the tip is raised and lowered to keep this tunnelling current constant. The instrument is so sensitive that the tip has to be raised and lowered to pass over individual atoms, and, as it moves up and down, the brightness or colour of the image changes. The microscope 'sees' atoms as arrays of adjacent spheres, rather like oranges packed in a crate.

Interestingly, it was another scanning instrument, the scanning electron microscope that uses a tiny beam of electrons rather than a metal tip, that we used to fabricate the 8-nanometre wire in 1976, and Ernst Ruska, the designer of the first electron microscope, shared the Nobel Prize with Binnig and Rohrer. In terms of ultimate capability, the STM was able to place individual atoms, which are some forty times smaller than the 8-nanometre wire, so it might be thought that the STM would be an ideal tool for fabricating electronic devices, and that it would immediately make it possible to make transistors with atomic proportions. Unfortunately, this is not the case; the process of placing atoms is far too slow to be economically practicable.

In contrast, the microlithography process that I described earlier is immensely fast. A modern microlithography camera exposes in one second a pattern that contains the elements of billions of transistors. The pattern has the complexity of a million high-definition television images, so the camera has an effective exposure rate of about a trillion pixels per second. It is because billions of transistors are produced simultaneously that they become individually so cheap. The cost of a transistor has been reduced by a factor of more than 10 million times since I was an undergraduate in Melbourne in the 1950s. To expose a pattern of this complexity using the same technique used to place single atoms in the STM would take tens of thousands of years. To overcome this constraint, researchers have been using arrays of thousands of tips to increase speed, but so far the shortfall in writing speed remains immense. This is a classic example of the difficulty often encountered in bridging between science and technology. Technology by necessity must be practicable and economically sensible. With science, discovery is sufficient.

The next thread in the tapestry had its origins in mechanical engineering, in the ability to make precise components for a wide variety of products. It was in effect the skill underlying watch-making more than two centuries ago. In recent times the precision required in the components of jet engines, car engines, electric motors, cameras, telescopes, etc., has reached the nanometre level. To meet this demand, machines such as lathes and milling machines have themselves become examples of nanometre precision. Lathes have their cutting tools positioned with laser interferometers that are accurate to nanometres, and the cutting edges are made from diamond so that they do not wear. Laser-controlled diamond machining in effect became a nanotechnology more than twenty years ago, and as such was one of the earlier of the new array of technologies to do so.

Another early example of the use of nanometre-size elements was catalysis, where nanometre particles are used to 'catalyse' chemical processes. A well-known example is the catalytic converter used in car exhaust systems that has been so effective in reducing the pollution produced by vehicle engines. There are many other areas where the boundaries between chemistry, chemical engineering and nanotechnology disappear.

The next series of threads arose from what had previously been known as thin film technology. It has long been possible to deposit, or grow, very thin films on surfaces to improve the properties of the surface for a variety of purposes, for example to increase resistance to corrosion and wear. Such films have been used extensively on the metal components of engines of all kinds, producing great increases in life-time and performance. Thin films on window glass reflect the sun's rays and keep buildings cool in summer, or reject contaminants and keep the windows clean. Pilkington's self-cleaning glass is a striking example of what can be achieved. Thin film coatings have been used for almost a hundred years on the elements of lenses used in microscopes, telescopes, binoculars and cameras where they reduce scattered light by eliminating reflections and thereby increase the contrast in the image. Very often these thin layers are less than 1,000 nanometres in thickness and hence their use can correctly be called a nanotechnology.

Another large group of threads arose from materials science, especially composite materials. Composite materials have been around for decades, but recently the fibres and particles that are embedded in these materials have become small enough to be classed as nanostructures and hence the whole subject becomes a nanotechnology. The outstanding examples in this category are the carbon fibre reinforced materials, especially those that use carbon nanotubes that are only a few nanometres in diameter, and the sun screens that include nanometre particles to increase the absorption of ultra-violet radiation.

It is in the use of these nanoparticles and nanotubes that concern has most plausibly been expressed about the risks and dangers of nanotechnology. It is suggested that these particles may enter living cells more easily than larger particles and trigger unforeseen processes, and it is known that particles of this size may be more active chemically than larger particles of the same material. The air is full of nanometre-sized particles which we breathe in and out all the time, but past experience teaches us to be cautious. Asbestos, cigarette smoke and carbon particles emitted by diesel engines come to mind. The two particular nanoparticles that have gained attention are titanium oxide nanoparticles that have been used in sun screens to filter out damaging ultra-violet radiation; and carbon nanotubes that may be used in composite materials to add strength, or as elements in electronic devices.

The recent report of the Royal Academy of Engineering and the Royal Society on Nanoscience and Nanotechnologies recommends that these nanoparticles should be carefully monitored, which would seem to be a very sensible precaution and I am pleased that it has gained wide support. The report does not see other areas as posing threats and even with nanoparticles there is no risk when the particles are embedded rather than discrete. It would seem wise to me to be cautious about the use of any new materials, whether of nanometre size or not, especially when they are to be brought into contact with people and animals.

There is another aspect of nanotechnology that has gained a lot of attention as a potential threat but which is perhaps at most speculative and unproven. This is molecular manufacturing, which is the name given to the concept of using an 'assembler' to build up structures atom by atom to form molecular machines. It has been suggested by the proponent of this technology, Eric Drexler, that these machines could replicate in an uncontrollable manner to form what has been called 'grey goo'. But to date there has been no experimental verification that such machines could be built or that there are mechanisms by which they could replicate. There are not even proven ways to model such structures. As the above-mentioned report said, 'Our experience with chemistry and physics teaches us that we do not have any idea how to make an autonomous self-replicating machine at any scale.'

There are of course biological systems that do

replicate, and some of these, such as the bacterial viruses, are about 100 nanometres in size. However, they have to attach to a bacterium in order to replicate and we are far from understanding the details of the way in which they do this.

Which leads me to the group of threads that surprised me most when it became part of the nanotechnology tapestry: the group that has its roots in biochemistry and molecular biology. But, having accepted that nanotechnologies were to do with structures and phenomena that have nanometre dimensions, as indeed we suggested more than thirty years ago, I should not have been surprised. DNA molecules and proteins have dimensions of nanometres and, as molecular biologists can manipulate the molecular structure of proteins and DNA, they can surely call themselves 'nanotechnologists', should they wish to do so.

But at this point I feel that the descriptive net may have been spread too far, and I have only had time to mention a selection of threads that make up the tapestry of nanotechnology and nanoscience – others include the micro-electro-mechanical devices

(MEMS), especially sensors, ceramics, light-emitting diodes, nanofiltration membranes, drug discovery, compact disks, and on and on. Inclusion of molecular biology along with all of these means that nanotechnology covers almost all modern technologies, and the term becomes so unspecific that its usefulness is limited and it can be confusing to people.

However, there are clearly advantages to the adoption of the labels 'nanotechnology' and 'nanoscience'. There is the excitement created by what is a new and exciting group of technologies, even if individually its members had perfectly satisfactory names, and those that take on the title gain the glamour of the most successful, and more importantly make themselves eligible for any funding that is allocated by government and private sources. On the other hand, it is unfortunate for the majority of nanotechnologies that they should be linked with the potential dangers of the few that involve discrete nanoparticles, or with the unrealistic speculation that has accompanied nano-robots and self-replication.

Centuries ago, the watchmaker and instrument-maker with his eye-glass was working at the limit of then-available technology, in fabricating mechanisms which could hardly be seen by the naked eye. His was the technique which prefigured the almost infinitely smaller technologies of today that have been enabled by the broad range of new microscopes and analytical tools.

But to go back to where I started, I celebrate the fact that, as the last century came to a close, we saw the small catch up with the large in terms of practical significance to the human race. It would have been difficult to persuade Brunel that the ability to design and fabricate at the nanometre scale was going to have as much impact upon people as the ability to build bridges and railways, but I believe that this is now the case. Humankind stands to benefit as much – or more – from the brilliant array of nanotechnologies I have described as it did from the giant engineering achievements of a century or more ago.

5

Risk and responsibility

Almost exactly ninety-three years ago, on 15 April 1912, over 2,000 terrified and bewildered people found themselves, with little warning, drifting or drowning in the ice-cold North Atlantic. Only 712 of them survived that night. They were, of course, the passengers, officers and crew of the White Star steamship *Titanic*, and they were in a sense victims of 'failures' of technology.

The *Titanic* disaster was in the main a result of over-reach, of a gap between the achievements of some technologies and the shortcomings of others; and of managerial failures on the part of those who used the available technology. Although *Titanic* had a radio communications system – and it was an important factor in directing rescue vessels to her – it was a system still in its infancy. Although the technology of shipbuilding already embraced double skins and water-tight bulkheads, these fell far short of the completeness that we now expect. Those navigating this huge vessel were in some important respects no further advanced than the Vikings who had sailed these same seas ten centuries before: they could locate themselves only by means of stellar observation and dead reckoning, and they had only their eyes to see what lay ahead – and this was less than a hundred years ago.

The managerial failures were perhaps worse. The ship's officers were warned of ice by radio messages, which they ignored. They hadn't carried out safety drills or trained the ship's company. The ship was speeding blindly into a known danger area in order to meet her scheduled arrival time in New York. Accidents, by definition, happen. But more diligent officers, properly trained crew, and a sufficiency of lifeboats could have saved the majority of those lost to the depths on that dreadful April night.

What does this long-ago catastrophe have to say to us today? It's from such appalling experiences, avoidable perhaps only with hindsight, that we learn how to progress more safely, and it is this process of trial and error by which medicine, aviation, safety in transportation have been transformed in the lifetimes of many of us.

If technology is to continue to triumph, however, and I am convinced that the future well-being of our planet and all its inhabitants requires that it should, then technologists must seriously address themselves to the fundamental issues bearing on their work What we must *not* do is either complacently ignore risks, as the managers of the White Star Line did before 1912, or submit unthinkingly to false terrors of their possible consequences. There has been great progress in making our lives safer, and my hope is that over the next century we may achieve as much progress for the planet we live in. After all, our lives and those of generations to come depend on the health of our environment.

In this final chapter I am making a green argument. As a technologist this should not be surprising, but because of the gap in understanding that has developed, it may be beyond the grasp of many people to realise that the solutions to the problems created by technology will themselves be technological. What we engineers have to do is to be seen to have codes of acceptable behaviour and to be living up to those standards. And we must communicate more and better, be more transparent in what we do, and be prepared patiently to debate public concerns, even if we believe that these concerns are based upon prejudice or ignorance. It is time now as a matter of urgency and for the sake of saving our planet, and thus safeguarding the future of the human race, to move away from the old concept of 'the public understanding of science' to a new more dynamic 'public engagement'. We must work harder to understand what troubles the public, and anticipate the technological developments that are likely to be of concern.

It is not just the engineers and scientists that are to blame. Intelligent public debate demands a broader understanding on the part of everybody, and standing in the way of this broader understanding is the specialisation encouraged by our schooling system. It is still possible, in England at least, for young people from the age of fifteen to study only mathematics and physics, or on the other hand to do no science or mathematics at all. Let engineers and scientists learn

their Shakespeare and play the violin; and arts graduates should be ashamed rather than proud to be igno-
rant of technology. And we still have much to do on
gender balance.

I make no distinction between someone who does
not know the difference between electric current and
voltage, and someone who knows nothing of Byron.
Why is it that we accept the former and regard the
latter as a Philistine? Neither is satisfactory; we
should strive for a cultural balance. We need those
with understanding of history and the arts to enable
technology to be used for good. In our schools, girls
now outperform boys in all subjects, and yet most
girls are frequently brought up to assume that engineering and many of the sciences are male subjects.
The wasted potential is vast.

In an earlier chapter I talked about the industrial
revolution that occurred in the closing decades of the
last century as globalisation became practicable and
products were assembled from the world's best
components, no matter where they were made. There
was also a revolution in our understanding of the
need to do things in a way that preserved our

precious resources. Advanced instrumentation brought us data on the condition of the biosphere, and we became aware of the damage that was being done to the ozone layer and the effects of excessive production of carbon dioxide.

Engineers reacted to these data with a plethora of potential solutions, just as they did in the 1960s when air pollution in the world's largest cities reached unacceptable limits and anti-pollution devices were needed for cars. But the situation now, as then, is not simply technological. Solutions require political decisions that depend on public debate and bring us back to the question of public engagement.

Let me start with travel. I travel a lot, as many of us do – probably too much for the sake of the planet. For example, I am conscious every time I fly to the Far East, or Australia, and back that one ton of aviation fuel is consumed for myself and each one of my fellow passengers – and that assumes that the plane is full. This is bad enough but at least the fuel is used to carry passengers to their destinations and is not wasted. This is not the case for the fuel wasted while planes circle airports waiting to land, or queue up on the ground, waiting to take off. This profligate waste is a result of the inability of our public decision-making processes to implement in time what our business and technical experts have been telling us for years about the growth in airline traffic. Technology is the great leveller. It is allowing more and more people to enjoy what was once only for the wealthy. We need to accept these trends and improve our ability to provide environmentally friendly solutions.

The situation with our road traffic is even worse. It is estimated that the cost of traffic congestion in the UK is £15 billion per year, the highest cost per capita in Europe. But the cost is not the only issue. Almost all the road vehicles have their engines running while they are stopped in traffic jams, wasting fuel and polluting the atmosphere. This is another example of the lack of adequate planning and acceptance of the projections of experts. Several First-World countries have built railways that are clear winners in terms of time and convenience for journeys up to about 500 miles. According to Professor Roger Kemp of Lancaster University, domestic airline flights use more than three times the energy of a Shinkansen train running at 275 km/hour, and the train's energy can be produced by non-polluting sources, such as wind turbines and nuclear power, rather than fossil fuels. It is clear that we should not be encouraging the expansion of short-haul air travel, especially as research has shown that emissions at a high altitude are much more damaging to the environment than emissions at ground level.

Our means of generating and consuming energy are also unnecessarily wasteful. Let me start with consumption. Our houses are poorly insulated and sealed and our building regulations inadequate. Average householders have little idea how much energy they are using, or how they could reduce their consumption. Many do not even read their consumption meters themselves, and a huge number pay estimated bills because no one is reading the meters on a regular basis. Technology could supply simple solutions to this difficulty, for example by providing meters that could be located in kitchens, or over back doors, that gave the householder a real-time indication of the amount of power they were using – in terms of money and greenhouse gas production – and by enabling people to see immediately the effect of turning off unnecessary appliances. The cost of such meters would not be high as they would be trivial in complexity compared, for example, to a £50 DVD recorder.

When it comes to power generation, we have at least made some progress. We have realised that we are producing excessive quantities of carbon dioxide and that we need to switch to technologies that are sustainable. But a lack of realism remains in terms of how much this will cost, and how long it will take to implement. Much progress has been made with wind, wave and tidal generators but these technologies are not free from controversy and it is unlikely that they can provide more than about a fifth of our power requirements in the next twenty years, and even then the cost is likely to be much higher than, for example, present natural-gas-fired generators.

We need not be in this situation. France already generates 90% of its power in a greenhouse-gas-free manner – 77% nuclear and 13% hydro. We are going to have to reexamine the nuclear option. There has been great progress since we built our present nuclear plants, not only in the technology of generation but also in the disposal of nuclear waste. I am pleased that we are examining the options for nuclear waste in a process that does engage the public. But public assessment of risk, and trust – or lack of trust – in technologists have nevertheless brought us to an impasse that endangers our planet. The growth of naive green politics is itself endangering future generations as we reject further investigation of technological solutions, such as nuclear power and genetically modified foods, that could perhaps save us – which brings me to the whole subject of the public's understanding of risk and how this has changed in recent times.

We have only to consider the central role of electricity in our society to see how wide-ranging risks have developed. Our dispersed, personal use of electricity is dependent on a single, highly centralised system that may be victim to natural or malign attack and is jeopardised by the depletion of fuel reserves. The responsibilities on the shoulders of engineers are huge. Explaining and understanding those risks is, I believe, a paramount necessity. For who amongst us will accept power failures, which not only plunge us into darkness but shut down our heating, refrigeration and communications systems and put at risk most of our transport and medical support systems? And yet security of supply is seldom quoted as a primary need when we enter the emotional debates about sustainable sources of power.

These are not only issues for our comfortable First World. The most idealistic amongst us will surely accept that application of some technologies is the likeliest, even the only, means by which the endemic poverty, disease and desperation in which a majority of the world's population live can be alleviated.

But the risks of pollution and contamination are not straightforward. If we are to realise acceptable worldwide reductions in the production of carbon dioxide and pollution, the developing world needs to join the developed world in changing to sustainable technologies. Without help they cannot do this – they have neither the technology nor the money and there is little sense in the rich world banning processes and procedures and imposing a heavy and expensive burden of regulation even if it had the power to do so.

The controversies I have mentioned involve

established technologies. Ethical issues become still more complex when associated with new technologies and processes. The pace of innovation and change is astonishing. A celebrated reference in a history of science written in 1964[1] points out that 'if this book were planned according to the volume of scientific discovery, everything before 1800 would be contained on the first page'. Bearing in mind the developments of the last forty years, that first page of summary would now be reduced to one paragraph. New technologies provide immense opportunities, but also undeniable risks, and open the question as to whether their development should be regulated.

In my opinion it is better for companies, institutions, universities to develop their own sets of ethical guidelines, rather than for governments to regulate. I recognise, however, that commercial pressures can lead to unacceptable behaviour and there are instances where governments do have to regulate. But they should do so reluctantly and only after engagement with the public. We need fast advances

1   It was A. R. Hall and M. B. Hall, *A Brief History of Science*, New York, 1964.

to deal with our problems and over-regulation is itself a risk to our future.

And when it comes to risk, everyone would benefit from a better understanding. We should all think more about how we decide what is acceptable risk. Why are some afraid to fly but happy to drive a car despite its hugely higher risk of injury or death, and perversely to drive aggressively and dangerously? Why do we accept a greater likelihood of accident at home than we do at work? These are some of the key questions discussed in a series of reports of the Royal Academy of Engineering that have generated debate and hopefully will aid in rational decision making.

One crucial recommendation emerges: that the investigation of accidents should concentrate on finding the cause of the accidents not the person or persons to blame. The latter only leads to defensiveness and cover-up. The investigation should seek the cause of the accident so that it may be eliminated in the future. The airline industry's remarkable safety record is thought by some to be because the investigators seek the cause of accidents rather than hunt down the person to blame.

Now as I conclude this volume, I want to indulge in the most dangerous of activities – the prediction of what technology is likely to achieve in the years ahead. And you should be aware that we technologists frequently overestimate what will happen in the next five years, while completely missing the revolutions that can occur in twenty years. I have chosen just three areas in which I believe and hope that technology will continue to triumph and to change our lives dramatically.

The first is in our ability to solve larger and larger problems – for example to improve our ability to forecast the weather, to control national or regional economies better, to design more effective drugs, or to improve the management of highly complex organisations, for example hospitals or even health systems, or entire complex businesses, even to control and automate traffic flow. The challenge is to create even larger and more complex computer systems of the type that at present have such a mixed reputation, with many ending in fiasco as schedules slip and budgets overrun. I believe that slowly but certainly we are learning from our mistakes and are going to succeed in many of these endeavours – 95 per cent accuracy in weather forecasting, hospitals in which mistakes are almost never made, the alleviation of poverty, further reductions in accident rates on the roads and railways. This is a glimpse of what we might be able to do.

Technology will increasingly be able to identify objects and people. Success with radio frequency tags may eliminate the manual check-out in our supermarkets and shops; keys and money as we know them will become curiosities of the past; and we will enjoy more security for ourselves and our possessions. These of course raise serious matters for public engagement.

The final area of advance will be in medical technologies, not an area in which I am expert, but one where I am confident that vast strides will be made – in the control of, and perhaps even in the curing of, AIDS and some forms of cancer; and in the creation of prosthetics, such as hip and knee joints, that will last a lifetime, perhaps through the nanostructuring of their surfaces, as I learned at Glasgow University when I was delivering the last Reith lecture there. All these and many more are giving rise to remarkable increases in life expectancy and this is expected to continue, with significant social consequences.

No matter where we look, technology is changing and shaping our lives. I hope I have convinced you in the last five chapters that technology is our friend. We must engage with it as a society and use it to push forward. In the last century we learned a great deal from our disasters, and hugely increased the number of people enjoying the myriad benefits of technology. Now we are at risk of permanently endangering our planet. Our aim for this century should be to make comparable progress in protecting our environment. Technology will surely triumph if we succeed.

By way of conclusion

In the lectures from which the preceding five chapters have been transcribed, I outlined the emergence of technologies from simple beginnings, sometimes through a process of chance and luck, to the situation at the beginning of the twenty-first century, where highly complex equipment and techniques are accessible to all. I went on to ask how such advances can be sustained and what the dangers are to which we must be alert. Each of the lectures was followed by a discussion, part of which was broadcast, and during these discussions, and in subsequent correspondence, several general themes emerged. These were so interesting that they prompted me in this final section to elaborate on some of the points that I made during the lectures in the light of the comments made by listeners.

The first of these topics generated much debate,

and although it was originally a fairly minor point it reveals what I believe to be an important gap in public understanding. Earlier in the year the public had voted for the 'safety bicycle' as Great Britain's most valuable invention, and I referred to this as an illustration of what I thought to be a general lack of appreciation of the range and sophistication of modern technology. It is not that I underestimate the technical and sociological importance of John Starley's 1885 invention. This was not, of course, the first bicycle but it was the first to be taken up as an everyday means of transportation. Starley's advance was to use two sprockets of different sizes joined by a chain, so that the driven wheel rotated faster than the pedals, thereby allowing that wheel to be smaller, in fact to have two wheels of equal size and an easily mountable frame. We all recollect museum examples and illustrations of the two-metre-tall 'penny-farthing' bicycle, which appears to us such a bizarre contraption. But its logic was that the huge front wheel was directly pedaled, and therefore had to be much larger so as to transform the rotation of the pedals into speeds faster than walking pace. The penny-farthing was in fact a forebear of the speedway bicycle, and was intrinsically unsuitable for anyone other than the young racers of its day. Starley's bicycle was far more practicable and – combined with pneumatic tyres – led to much more widespread use of the bicycle, with significant social consequences. Like almost all successful technological advances, it became a great leveller and allowed people who could not afford other means of transport to gain a mobility that had previously been beyond their reach. It particularly contributed to the independence of women. His bicycle has stood the test of time and its basic design principles survive in very much the same form today. It also proved to be more energy efficient than any other form of transport and to be the ultimate in environmental friendliness.

Notwithstanding its important consequences, I still maintain that this British invention is less significant than, perhaps above all others, Michael Faraday's crucial demonstration of the principles underlying the generation of electric current. Faraday showed that when a wire coil was moved through a magnetic field a current was sustained in the coil and that this current could be used to power electric devices. Electric currents are now employed in almost every device we use. All modern communications and most entertainment depend upon it: the telephone, radio, cinema, television, and more recently computers and the Internet. Electricity is central to the control and drive systems of all forms of transportation and to most manufacturing. The medical instrumentation which has transformed our diagnostic skills and healthcare depends on electricity: scanners, heart monitors, X-ray and ultrasound equipment, and suchlike. The achievements go far beyond a conventional view of the direct role of electricity in illumination and propulsion: another advance of comparable significance, the discovery by Crick, Watson and Franklin of the structure and role of DNA, would itself have been impossible without electric power. The list of electricity's results is almost endless and their consequences have changed every aspect of our lives. Faraday's initial discovery has been built upon by hundreds of other creative minds until a mountain of intellectual achievement towers far above Starley's ingenious use of sprockets and a chain. That is my point, not to disparage Starley's important and inspired invention, but to place it in its context alongside this huge mountain of technical achievement stemming from a single simple principle first revealed 173 years ago.

The second topic that generated debate is not unrelated. It is the role of the individual in the creative process. I said that individuals working in isolation could make little contribution to advancing the complex modern technologies that are built upon these volumes of previous intellectual achievement. This is not to say that individuals cannot come up with ideas that will have impact – just as Faraday and Starley did – or ideas that will be sufficient in themselves to generate new and successful businesses. It is the second qualification, that of working in isolation, which is the key to my statement. Almost all truly innovative advances by definition come from individuals, but with the growth in complexity of new technologies it is only those who have developed true insight into the workings of a new technology that are in a position even to know whether their ideas are significant. And it is only through extensive knowledge of all that has already been accomplished that one can gain such an insight.

I remember as a young engineer dreaming that I would invent a transistor that would be faster than anyone else's. In my undergraduate lectures in the 1950s I had been told that transistors would never operate faster than about 1 million Hertz (that is, cycles per second) and that they were unlikely ever to be useful in, for example, televisions, where much higher frequencies were required. What a coup it would be to prove that this was wrong. I had no idea how I would accomplish this but I thought that perhaps I would wake up in the night with a novel idea that would provide the solution. I know now how naive and foolish this was. This is not the process. I had first to become an expert, to understand the intimate details of transistor design, and to learn about the many and complex factors that limit transistor speed. It was not sufficient just to understand how the transistor operated and to think that I would eventually, through serendipity, find a way to shorten the distance the electrons had to travel and thereby increase the transistor's speed. I had to start to climb the intellectual peak, like planning one's way up a difficult mountain, first deciding which ridge I would tackle and then working on the skills that I would need to handle that particular approach. Having gained this knowledge, then at least I was in a position for those magical processes of creativity to work in my brain, so that when I woke up in the middle of the night with a new idea, it would be one that was relevant to the problem. I might at least be able to push back one of the barriers that was limiting the speed.

But there is still more complexity. Just increasing the speed of the transistor would not be sufficient because the circuit in which it was to operate would in all likelihood no longer be adequate. I would have to work with those who had already climbed that circuit design mountain to find a way usefully to employ my new transistor. And then I would need to consult the engineers who were designing the systems that the circuit would be used in – the radio, television, computer, ignition control system, satellite navigation system – to see if the circuit or transistor would be of any use to them. Without all these connections my efforts as an individual working on the transistor would have been a waste of time. Working as an isolated individual I would never have been able to make a significant contribution.

It is not necessary to work in a large organisation to be successful but it is necessary to be familiar with the broader technological world. There are some remarkable examples of how individuals with insight have started relatively small companies, and have taken on the giants and been truly successful in competing with them. Two examples in my own field of electronics immediately come to mind: Ray Dolby who founded Dolby Laboratories, a company that has competed with remarkable success in the highly competitive field of audio engineering; and Robin Saxby's ARM, a company that now dominates in the field of low-power microprocessors for use in portable electronic devices, especially mobile phones.

It is also the case that, in some respects, an individual now has greater opportunities to contribute than was once the case, because the old isolation – geographical as well as political and economic – which once excluded those outside a small charmed circle has been broken down by the communications and information systems of the electronic age. The contribution of the Internet to this process cannot be overstated.

The education of the creators of technology, the engineers and scientists, drew considerable comment from listeners, many of whom were dismayed at the decline in the proportion of young people opting for these careers. Many reasons were cited, but the most frequent was the lack of an adequate reward at the end of what can be a long and difficult university education. This perception is not borne out by reality, as the average salaries for young engineers are amongst the highest of all of the professions, but it must be said that exceptional graduates are not paid exceptionally as they are in the financial and consulting sectors, and this is a grave mistake on the part of industry. It is the genius of the design engineer that determines the success of so many products.

Many people expressed the belief that, ironically, today's technology gets in its own way in attracting young people. Modern products have become so sophisticated and complex that a young engineer can do little even to maintain them, let alone to modify or create them. The young become frustrated and bored with the artificial world of models and are deprived of a useful outlet for their burgeoning abilities. When I was a child, I had the joy of making my own radio, starting with a crystal set. This was the only way I could possibly have owned a radio. A crystal set only cost a few weeks' pocket money whereas a ready-made radio cost twenty times as much. In building the crystal set, I not only had the satisfaction of learning how it worked, but the material benefit of owning it. Now, a radio with many times the functions of a crystal set costs less than the components for a crystal set, so that the exercise of building it yourself is completely deprived of usefulness.

Cars are another example. Only a few decades ago, there were many who could only afford a car if they understood enough to maintain and repair it. Young people with these skills could own a car, those who didn't, could not. The electronic systems that control the workings of a modern car do not encourage amateur intervention, eliminating the privilege of the knowledgeable, even for those who understand the electronic systems. Modern cars are more reliable, however, meaning they seldom need maintenance, and because modern technologies allow more to be accomplished with less, they are more affordable, so the trend is irreversible. None the less, the inaccessibility still deprives the owner of a sense of usefulness and involvement.

The next topic concerned many in the audiences and was expressed in a variety of ways. There were some who felt strongly the need to control, or even to halt, the future development of technology because of the growing damage it is thought to have caused, and the perceived dangers that it presented for the future. Such opinions emerged especially in the context of the harm that has been done to the earth and its atmosphere by the excessive use of energy. There is now widely accepted and reliable evidence that carbon dioxide is accumulating in the earth's atmosphere and that this may lead to an irreversible warming process with disastrous consequences for our climate and everything related to it. Environmental pollution has many aspects, and they include topics removed from our present subject, such as the destruction of forests and the degradation of the seas. But the two areas of pollution most susceptible to technical amelioration – just as the problems themselves arise from technical processes – are power generation and transportation. Not surprisingly, these topics caused much discussion. This is a topic which I raised in the final lecture when I called for immediate action to reverse present trends. I return to it again now to outline in greater detail the options that we have to reduce the production of carbon dioxide, and especially the issue of whether we need to consider the building of new nuclear power plants. At present, I see no alternative to keeping the nuclear option open if we are to meet our immediate obligations to protect the environment.

But I want to emphasise that the maintenance or enlargement of nuclear capacity is not sufficient in itself. It needs to be part of a wider process which both vigorously promotes energy conservation and develops renewable methods of generation. Nuclear energy must complement, not substitute for, renewable sources. I have already described the central place which electric power plays in every aspect of our lives. The paramount need to ensure security of supply, and to avoid fuel poverty, means that we shall have to consider all alternatives, especially the renewables, but not excluding a continuing role for nuclear generation.

We have been fortunate in the United Kingdom because in our 'dash for gas', we succeeded, almost by accident, in meeting our commitment under the UN Framework Convention on Climate Change – by 2000 we had already returned to 1990 levels of greenhouse gas emissions. Although the total electricity supplied in the UK by all generators in 2004 was 2% higher than in 2003, the fuel used was 0.9% lower. Since February 2005, however, the Kyoto Protocol commits the EU to a further 8% reduction between 2008 and 2012, and again the UK has committed to do more. We, in Britain, have courageously agreed to a domestic goal of 20% reduction by 2010. These are laudable aims but provisional data for total UK emissions of carbon in 2004, whilst 4.2% lower than 1990, show a 1.5% increase over 2003. It is also worth noting that our domestic gas production is declining as the UK Continental Shelf reserves deplete, and indeed we became a net importer of gas in 2004, for the first time since 1996. With increased demand, it is expected that we will be importing 80% of our gas by 2020.

Energy efficiency measures are widely thought likely to be the cheapest and safest way of meeting our goals. In addition the Government intends that by 2010 a tenth of our electricity should be generated from renewable sources, rising to one fifth by 2020. Yet the House of Lords Science and Technology Committee report 'Renewable Energy: Practicalities', prepared under the chairmanship of Lord Oxburgh, was not optimistic about the possibility of meeting these targets. It states: 'We found almost no-one outside Government who believed that the White Paper targets were likely to be achieved. This was partly for practical reasons – planning consents, availability of labour and equipment and so on – and partly as a direct consequence of the Renewables Obligation method of support. We judge that by 2010 the United Kingdom may have achieved 6–7% renewable generation.' It is also the case that renew-able sources are not themselves necessarily publicly acceptable nor pollution-free.

Such problems might potentially be solved in the long term by nuclear fusion, by replicating the thermonuclear reactions powering the sun, but even the most optimistic of experts say that this will take thirty years and the official timetable is closer to fifty. So we cannot rely on fusion to solve our near-term needs in terms of greenhouse gas reduction. However, we do have nuclear fission. Our experience of generating electricity from nuclear fission extends back to 1956. The technological problems are well understood and manageable but there are well-known issues, some sociological, some political, which will make it difficult to gain public and political acceptance for additional or replacement nuclear capacity.

Other than importing uranium fuel, the UK has been self-sufficient in employing nuclear fission, through plant design, operation, regulation, uranium enrichment, fuel fabrication, reprocessing and waste treatment. However, in 1995 the Government determined that, in the absence of finance from the private sector, nuclear power should be phased out and decommissioning begun. Draft legislation was published in mid-2003 to set up and fund the Nuclear Decommissioning Authority, which has now been established. It is this factor, the disposal of nuclear waste, which has created most public concern, but it is one which will have to be dealt with whether or not we build new nuclear plants. If we were to build ten new nuclear stations and operate them for sixty years, there would only be an increase in the UK's existing waste stockpile of about 10 per cent. It is also important to note that the waste arising from a modern Pressurised Water Reactor is much less than from the old Magnox gas-cooled reactors. The costs of decommissioning a light water reactor will also be five times less than that for a Magnox reactor, due to the smaller volume of material and graphite moderator.

Other countries are already alert both to dwindling sources of alternative power and to the need radically to address the waste disposal issue. For example, Finland decided in May 2002 to build a new nuclear reactor on economic, energy security and environmental grounds. Finland is also well advanced with provisions for the encapsulation and storage of spent fuel. They already operate underground repositories for intermediate-level waste and an underground rock characterisation facility will verify the site selection for geological storage over the next few years. Technical development and manufacture of such techniques is proceeding under contract in Great Britain. Sweden, on the other hand, remains committed to phasing out nuclear power, but, faced with the consequent electricity supply problems, public feeling is turning against this longstanding aspiration.

Transport contributes an increasing proportion of greenhouse gas pollution, mainly because of the huge and continuing growth in use of the internal combustion engine. Increased engine efficiency and cleanliness has been counteracted by the increased volume of car use in the developing world (especially China) and by a tendency towards larger and less fuel-efficient vehicles in wealthy countries (the 'SUV' phenomenon). Emissions from aircraft engines perhaps exemplify better than any other technological issue the gap between public aspirations and public behaviour. We all want to fly cheaply to the sun. But none of us wants new runways in our backyards and we would rather that the alarming increase in atmospheric pollution caused by aero engines did not take place. Similarly, a campaigning group recently attacked 'park-and-ride' schemes on the grounds that they used up the countryside and promoted car use. The balancing of such contending considerations is a central issue for the years ahead, but it is a debate which has to understand and embrace the technological issues and the potential of technology to solve the underlying questions. A solution necessarily involves some changes to life-style habits, and transport choices. Technology can be used to encourage such changes. For example, the British Government has signalled its interest in using sophisticated technology to introduce differential road-pricing to persuade people to share cars and discourage them from driving during peak congestion hours.

My final topic concerns the nature of corporate responsibility and its implications for the future control of technological development. Looking back over the long history of technical and industrial progress, no one would argue that social responsibility was a consideration until quite recent times. In part this was a matter of ignorance of the effects of processes, especially in such areas as pollution. Partly it was a consequence of haste and cost-cutting, as may have been the case in the Third World more recently. In our discussions, several listeners raised the question of trust, of whether large corporations will behave in a responsible manner, or whether they will do anything for commercial profit, regardless of its impact. I firmly believe that in this field, impelled it must be said by such appalling incidents as the Bhopal disaster (Union Carbide), and the dishonesty and greed of the senior officers in Enron, Worldcom and Tyco, civil society has won the battle of ideas. The corporate world today has largely embraced the principles of good citizenship, I believe irreversibly, and most corporations have a senior executive with explicit responsibility for developing and ensuring continuing social responsibility. Few would argue that this is wrong. Modern communications and the vigilance of the news media will police the matter effectively.

There are clearly areas where rigorous control is needed, such as in medicine, food quality and transportation safety. There may also be benefits in establishing universal standards in communication systems and building regulations. But I have argued that excessive use of controls imposed by government may be damaging and may even be counter-productive. This is not to say that the conduct of industry is no one's concern but the firm's, or that technical development should be left to proceed as it pleases. Public intervention is needed, and must be stringent. But there are already indications – and sensible observers are aware of examples – that regulation can become impractical, insensitive and overly prescriptive. It is a matter for continuing debate how the regulatory function is best carried out, whether by government, by independent regulators or by industry itself. But however it is done, it must be sensible and consistent, and not lay such burdens on the technologist and the development engineer that the process of innovation is stifled at birth.

Fear of the unlimited consequences of technological advance is not new. And in our occasional nostalgia for a simpler world before complex technologies existed, let us never forget the blight of poverty, disease, malnutrition and chronic disease which often beset traditional communities, as they continue to do in much of the world today. My fervent belief is that technology holds the key to sustaining our banishment of these ills, everywhere and for ever.

Printed in the United States
By Bookmasters